ARMOR

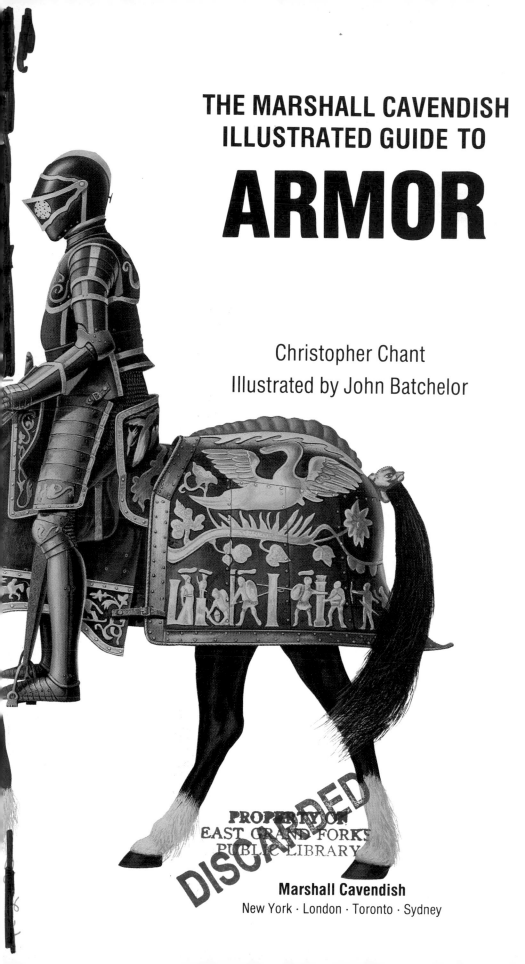

THE MARSHALL CAVENDISH ILLUSTRATED GUIDE TO

ARMOR

Christopher Chant

Illustrated by John Batchelor

Marshall Cavendish
New York · London · Toronto · Sydney

Library Edition 1989

© Marshall Cavendish Limited 1989
© DPM Services Limited 1989

Published by Marshall Cavendish Corporation
        147 West Merrick Road
        Freeport
        Long Island
        N.Y. 11520

Produced by DPM Services Limited
Designed by Graham Beehag
Illustrations © John Batchelor

Library of Congress Cataloging-in-Publication Data

Chant, Christopher.
    Armor/written by Chris Chant: Illustrated by John Batchelor.
      p.   cm—(The Marshall Cavendish illustrated guides)
    Includes index.
    Summary: An illustrated history of armor discussing its varied
designs and uses.
    ISBN 1-85435-089-7
    1. Arms and armor—Juvenile literature. [1. Arms and armor.]
I. Batchelor, John H., [1]. II. Title. III. Series: Chant,
Christopher. Marshall Cavendish illustrated guides.
U825.C47 1989
355.8'241—dc19   88-28761
                                          CIP
                                          AC

    ISBN 1-85435-085-4 (set).

Printed and bound in Italy by L.E.G.O. SpA, Vicenza

Man's first weapon was himself, a complex but adaptable shock system with feet to kick, hands to hold and hit, fingers to scratch and gouge, and teeth to bite. How and why men started to fight will never be known, but hand-in-hand with this tendency was the need to hunt. Here, man is limited by his comparatively low speed. To kill food animals before they could escape, he needed missile weapons (thrown weapons), and the first of them were probably stones and sturdy sticks. They could be used as conventional missiles (the stone as a projectile and the stick as a spear) or for hand-held shock weapons (as clubs). Sharpened antlers and other animal bones provided an alternative to stones and sticks. Millenia of slow evolution and the discovery of techniques such as flint-knapping to sharpen dull flints paved the way for new and more effective generations of weapons such as flint hand-axes, flint knives, and spears with flint blades: the first two could be upgraded with tied-on handles as axes

Armor has not always been full, as this Roman vase illustrates: on the left the gladiator with a short sword and shield has a helmet, arm and chest armor and one greave, while on the right his opponent with a net and trident appears to have only arm and shoulder armor.

5

The pourpoint was a close-fitting garment of padded leather, generally decorated with needlework. It was worn for comfort under armor in the 16th and 17th centuries and could be used as light protection when well padded.

Right: Egyptian soldiers were only lightly protected, sometimes with only a shield and a plaited arrangement of leather thongs on the chest to balance the offensive weapons.

and handled knives, and the latter with a spear-thrower for additional range. The next step was to adapt socketed stone or bone heads to provide effective maces for pounding, axes for chopping, daggers for thrusting, knives for cutting, swords for slashing, and, perhaps most important of all, bows to fire arrows (which were, in effect, small spears) with considerable force and accuracy over long ranges.

All of these were offensive weapons, probably first evolved for hunting. They were, however, inevitably used against other men. Man's ingenuity has often been brought to the fore by such challenges, and the threat posed by these weapons was met eventually with the development of personal protection. We call these defences "armor," it has been worn by all peoples with even the slightest pretensions to civilization. The development of armor has followed similar lines in all parts of the world, though not, of course, at the same time or to the same levels of technical skill.

Without a doubt, the first armor was made from the skins of animals, and such armor has been worn in the Philippines and other parts of Southeast Asia as recently as the memory of people living today. Tough hide is quite effective in halting or slowing down missile weapons, and in soaking up the energy of shock wea-

A relief at Karkemish shows a pair of heavily armed Hittite warriors with shields, spears, helmet and torso protection.

pons, especially if it is toughened by boiling or tanning. Such skins were initially worn as clothing, but only a short step was needed to develop shields (hide stretched over wooden frame) to prevent a weapon's effect from reaching the body at all. The addition of small pieces of wood or bone to the hide offered additional protection at the expense of weight, though the development of woven cloth allowed such platelets to be sewn onto a lightweight garment protecting the shoulders, chest, and stomach. Small plates or rings were initially attached to the outside of a garment, but later they were incorporated into the garment as the inside of a defensive "sandwich." This is called "brigandine armor," which was widely used in Europe between the 10th and 16th centuries.

A similar defense is offered by rods or slats of wood, or even bone, lashed together with cord or animal sinew. Such armor was widely used by the Indians of North and South America, and by the related races across the Bering Strait in northeastern Asia, but it

Above: Part of an 11th century ivory reliquary shows 6th century events (the conquest of the Cantabrigians by the Visigoths under King Leovigild), but the armor and helmet are typical of the mail of the 11th century.

Right: A detail from the Oseberg tapestry shows Viking warriors of the end of the 1st millenium, with simple helmets, mail coats and oval shields.

9

lacked flexibility and was generally restricted to a breastplate and/or backplate.

The discovery of metal transformed defensive armor. In the short term, the use of copper allowed the development, in a primitive form, of the brigandine armor mentioned above. It used the small, easily worked pieces of metal that were all that early metalsmiths could produce, and was thus comparatively cheap to produce, easy to maintain, and simple to repair. Copper was introduced in about 3500 BC, and was replaced in time by bronze (a strong alloy of copper and tin introduced to the eastern Mediterranean region in about 1700 BC by the Hyksos peoples from Mesopotamia) and finally by iron from about 1400 BC. The cost and difficult technologies associated with these substances prevented their use on a major scale, but the considerable strength and sharpness of bronze and iron was recognized in the military field.

There is little physical evidence (because of the "perishability" of these early alloys), but it seems likely that the next step in the development of armor from

A detail from an illustrated manuscript in Oviedo Cathedral in Spain shows the bodyguard of King Alfonso III, El Magno de Asturias, in the second half of the 9th century. Alfonso III was one of the first significant figures in the long process of expelling the Moors and Islam from Spain.

10

A romantic portrait of a
Viking chieftain, though it is
probably accurate in
suggesting that thick furs
were important to him as
much for protection from
weapons as from the cold.

the brigandine type was the elimination of cloth or hide in favor of garments made of linked rings: this "mail armor," or chain mail, was heavier than the brigandine type, but offered considerably more protection. It was probably combined with a cloth inner garment to reduce the discomfort of wearing the metal mesh, and this inner garment was probably padded to reduce the shock that was transmitted inward when a warrior was struck.

Plate armor offers better protection than chain mail, but is considerably heavier and far more demanding of the metalsmith's capabilities. It was also far more costly; bronze and iron were scarce, and therefore

The lance was generally between 10 and 14 ft long, with an average length of about 13 ft and diameter of 2 in increasing to 5 in on some tilting lances. Early lances were made of ash, but from the end of the 15th century, they were often made of aspen, cypress, pine, and sycamore.

Norman cavalry are depicted with some accuracy in the Bayeux Tapestry.

expensive and so used sparingly. It is thought that the Greeks were the first to make extensive use of plate armor, though their lack of tin for the creation of bronze was a constant limitation. In spite of that, his highly effective armor made the Greek soldier the decisive warrior of the period from about 700 to 300 BC. He had a helmet and shin-protecting greaves of plate construction, a large, basically circular shield and, in hoplite (heavy infantryman) form, a corselet to protect the torso. The corselet was often of ring or scale construction, and less frequently of plate, while the rest of the ensemble was plate. The overall effect was a high degree of protection without loss of mobility, which contributed to the success of the defensive and offensive operations waged by the Greeks against their most serious foes, the Persians. The hoplite concept reached its peak in the Macedonian armies of Philip and his son, Alexander the Great. Defensive armor remained essentially unaltered, and the success of these two superb generals stemmed from the organization and discipline of their forces in the face of numerically superior opponents.

The next stage in the improvement of defensive armor came with the Romans, who, over a period of 1,000 years from about 700 BC, built a huge empire that first consolidated Italy under Roman rule and then swept out to encompass all of western Europe, much of eastern and southeastern Europe, Asia Minor, the Middle East, and North Africa. Apart from the Romans' astute use of psychology and local politics to pave their way, the single most important factor in the Roman success was its regular army of highly trained and highly disciplined legionaries. These men conquered and held territory as it was "romanized" by the administrators who followed in their wake. Over the

The Europeans of the 1st Crusade defeated the Turks at Antioch in 1098, but this illustration shows later armor with a large proportion of plate.

Right: Purporting to show Robert the Bruce in 1306, a year before he became Robert I of Scotland, this illustration shows the famous man in armor of a later period.

Left: The Elector Maximilian of Bavaria (1573-1651) is shown wearing the fully developed armor of the first half of the 17th century.

Below: Though hardly realistic, illustrations such as these of knights closing for battle convey an immense sense of weight and slow movement.

centuries, the legionary was equipped with a variety of armor patterns, but they all centered on body armor, a helmet, and a shield, but no greaves or arm protection. Body armor was generally made of leather with bronze or iron reinforcement, though metal corselets were not unknown, and protection was given to the vulnerable hips and upper legs by the use of a "kilt" of metal-reinforced leather straps. The shield was particularly important; its classic form was virtually a half cylinder that protected the front and flanks. Lines of legionaries in close order presented the enemy with an immensely well-protected front, but one which could move with

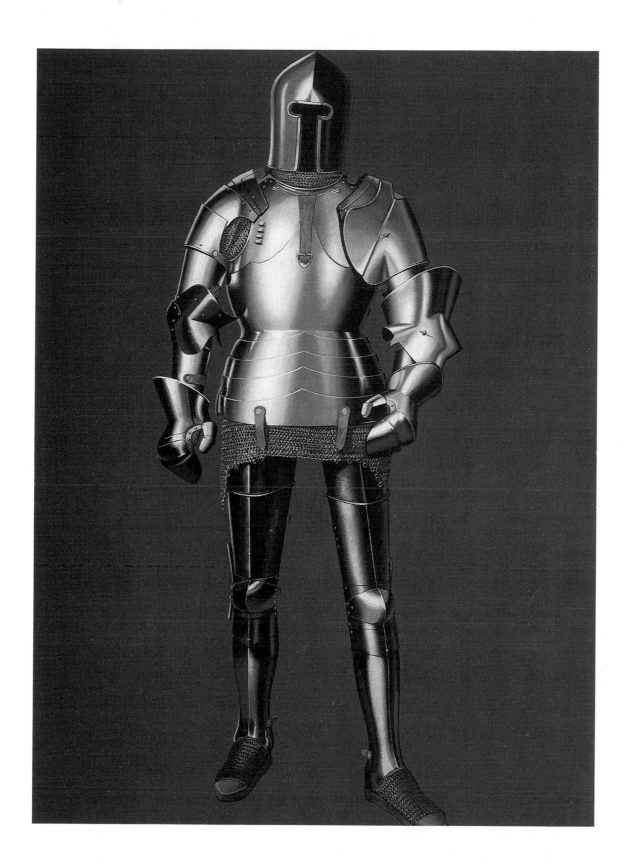

speed for great shock effect in the attack.

Where they survived, Rome's enemies tended to copy the basic features of Roman armor with changes to suit local practices and temperaments. The general style of Roman armor was kept by the tribes who overran the European portions of the Roman empire from the 4th century AD, though the following technological decline into the "dark ages" of the medieval period meant a loss in quality.

Improved armor began to appear in northern Europe at the beginning of the 10th century AD. Padded, scale, and ring armor were extensively used by the "ordinary" soldier, but chain mail became increasingly

18

19

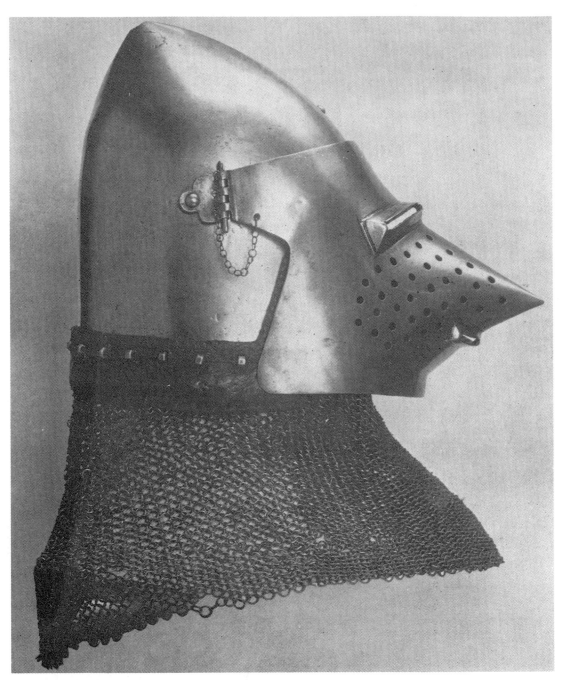

important for the aristocratic classes. It increasingly took the form of mail or quilted trousers and a mail coat with sleeves (hauberk) worn over a quilted undergarment (gambeson) to protect the wearer from the shoulders to the knees, including the arms as far as the elbows, and sometimes the wrists and even the hands

Above: **A visored basinet made in Milan (northern Italy) between 1390 and 1410.**

Half-armor provided protection for the head, torso, shoulders, arms, hands and thighs.

A basinet with hinged visor
and construction allowing the
main part of the helmet to be
opened out so that the wearer
could fit or remove the close-
fitting helmet without undue
difficulty.

with mail mittens. The overall level of protection provided by such armor was very high, while its weight
was light enough that it did not seriously hinder the
wearer on horse or on foot, especially as the hauberk
was split front and back below the waist. The ensemble was completed by the only piece of plate armor, a
pot helmet worn over a chain mail hood, itself worn
over a padded cloth hood.

The helmet was generally pointed and left the wearer's face uncovered. The Normans added a nasal, or bar that projected down to protect the nose, and the best known illustration of this type of armor is the Bayeux Tapestry, a huge embroidered panel depicting the invasion of southern England by William, Duke of

A complete set of Gothic man and horse armor, made in southern Germany between 1475 and 1485.

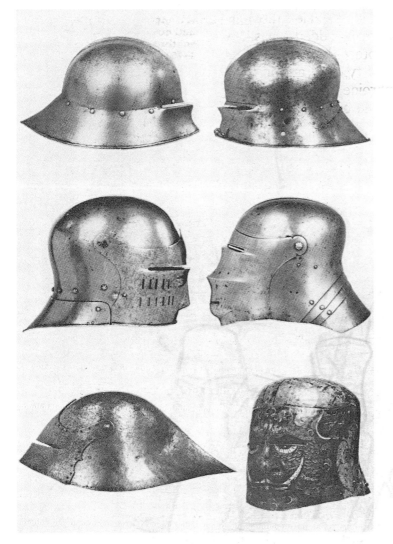

German salades of the period between 1450 and 1520. Note the "monster-faced" type at *bottom right*.

Normandy, and culminating in the Battle of Hastings in 1066 AD. Further development refined the Norman concept of mail armor, but until the 12th century, its development was limited by the inability of metalsmiths to produce and work larger pieces of plate. In the 12th century, the helmet began to undergo a change in shape. The first stage saw the development of larger helmets with flat tops and curved sides, generally known as "barrel helms." It was soon clear that the flat top was not sensible as it transmitted the force of any downward blow onto the head, and the barrel helm was soon replaced by the "sugar-loaf helm" with a pointed top to deflect the descending

Gauntlet is the name of the piece of armor covering the hands and wrists. Primitive gauntlets were made of leather and then chain mail, but the development of high-quality metalwork from the beginning of the 14th century allowed the steady development of plate gauntlets, of which later examples are still notable for the excellence of their workmanship and design in the jointed finger and thumb sections.

Fluted plate armor, made in Germany between 1510 and 1525, with the left shoulder of the tilting type.

blow and its force. This was a particuarly important factor, as the helm rested completely on the head, with none of its weight supported by the shoulders.

Increased iron-working capability and greater wealth allowed the upper classes to wear the gambeson with an enlarged suit of mail that reached to the ankles and enclosed the hands in mail gauntlets. Ordinary soldiers still had to make do with the gambeson, which was sometimes reinforced with pieces of mail or plate.

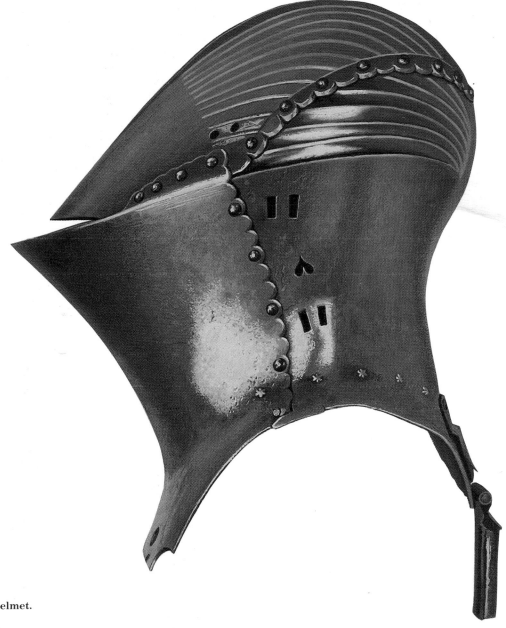

A fluted close-helmet.

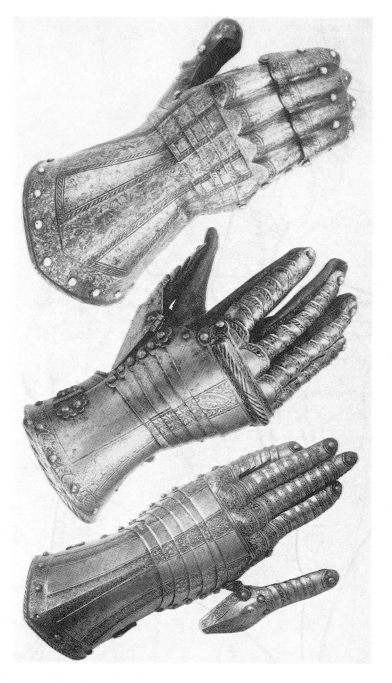

Some of the armorer's
greatest ingenuity was
displayed in the design and
manufacture of fully
articulated gauntlets
allowing the wrist, hand,
fingers and thumb to move
without serious hindrance.

By the last quarter of the 13th century, the refined skills and arts of the metalsmith made a major change in armor possible, which paved the way for a period of transition between the third quarter of the 13th century and the first quarter of the 15th century. In this period of about 130 years up to 1410, chain mail was

Etched half-armor, in the
Italian style, of the middle of
the third quarter of the 16th
century.

29

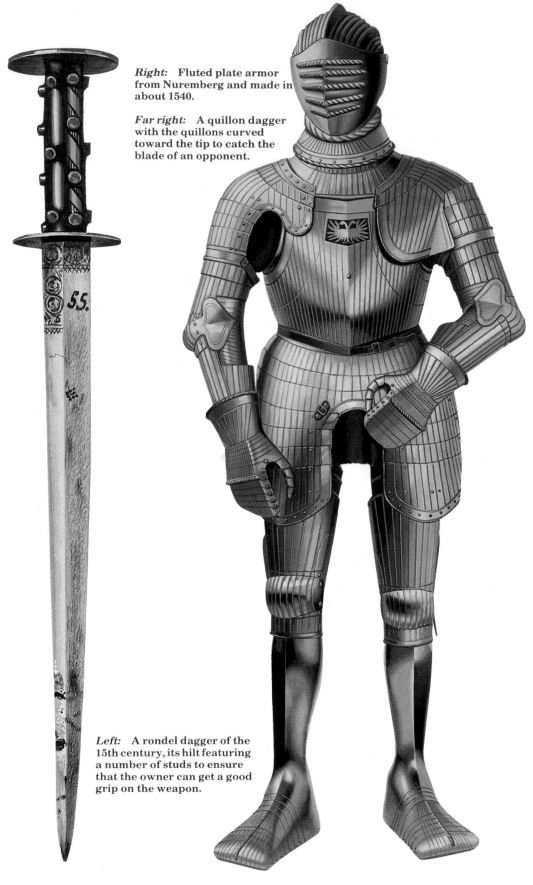

Right: Fluted plate armor from Nuremberg and made in about 1540.

Far right: A quillon dagger with the quillons curved toward the tip to catch the blade of an opponent.

Left: A rondel dagger of the 15th century, its hilt featuring a number of studs to ensure that the owner can get a good grip on the weapon.

increasingly reinforced and then replaced by plate. A stage in this process was the replacement of the mail hauberk by a brigandine type of protection for the torso with overlapping plates attached to the gambeson. The first step in the evolution from chain mail to plate armor was the knee cop of boiled leather and then plate, a hinged reinforcement for the knee. This was followed by the ailette, a flat shoulder protector laced to the hauberk or gambeson. The ailette had varying shapes and generally carried the owner's coat of arms. The next stage of evolution saw the provision of boiled leather or plate protection for the lower legs, and by the beginning of the 15th century, the process had reached the stage of replacing overall chain mail protection with overall plate protection. Forging skills had yet to reach the point at which fully articulating joints were possible, so the gaps between the plate sections were filled by sections of mail attached to the wearer's gambeson, which was still worn to provide at least some comfort and shock absorption between the plate and the knight wearing it.

Protection for the head had also been improved during this period. The Norman helmet had led to the barrel helm, in which the ear pieces were extended to meet the nasal and so protect the wearer's complete face: a slit was provided in front of the eyes so that the wearer had at least some vision, and breathing holes were frequently provided. This shape was developed into the sugar-loaf helm with a pointed rather than flat top, and at the time both types were known as heaumes (helms). The development of the metalsmith's art allowed the evolution of the helm into the great helm, in which the protection was continued downward in an extension that allowed the weight of this increasingly massive item to be carried on the wearer's shoulders. The helmet was frequently knocked off in battle, and this tendency was usefully reduced by the great helm, which was often attached to the backplate by a hasp and staple for extra security.

The great helm provided the wearer with greater protection, but it was extremely unwieldy. During the 14th century, it was replaced by the basinet, a lighter

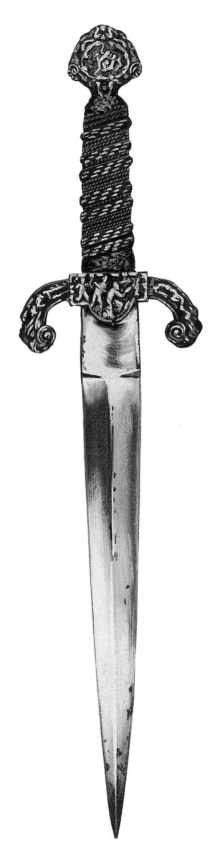

A Flemish or French embossed pageant shield of the mid-16th century. It carries the royal arms of France and shows the retreat of the English from Paris in 1523.

head covering developed from the close-fitting archer's skull cap by making the crown higher and deepening the sides and rear to protect the sides and back of the wearer's head. The basinet was worn over a chain mail hood, and by the middle of the 14th century, a rear flap of mail (the camail) had been added to protect the back of the neck and the shoulders. Extra protection for the face was provided by a triangle of mail attached to the front edges of the camail: it was hooked to the forehead when needed to cover the lower part of the face and the nose but leave the eyes exposed. In the third quarter of the 14th century, the basinet began to sprout a visor of the "pig-faced" or "dog-faced" variety. The visor generally came to a sharp forward point surrounded by breathing holes, and it had individual vision slits in front of the eyes. It was pivoted to swivel upward; early visors had pivots at the forehead, but the fully developed type had its pivots at the temple. Both pivots also featured hinges to allow the visor to be opened sideways or, by removing both hinge pins, removed entirely. In the first quarter of the

The heaviest known armor is that of William Somerset, 3rd Earl of Worcester, made at the Royal Workshop at Greenwich in 1570. It has five bulletproof sections which are interchangeable with less well-protected items; the suit weighs 81 lb 9 oz with the light sections, and 133 lb with the bulletproof sections.

Etched armor of about 1560, typical of the Italian school.

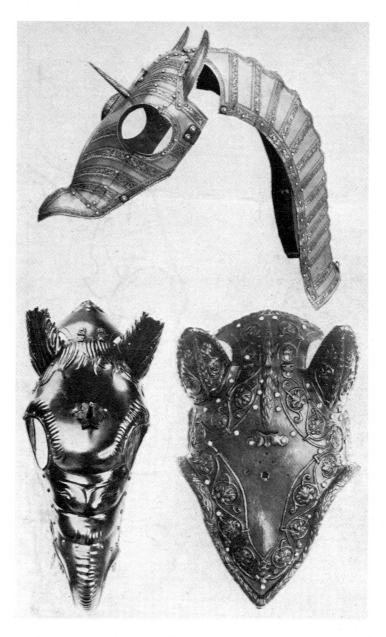

15th century, the camail was replaced by plated neck guards, and this great basinet was therefore supported by the shoulders.

By the beginning of the 15th century, complete plate armor was in use, and the century from 1510 may be regarded as the period of European Gothic plate armor. This period was marked by a painstaking development of armor in those details that matched its form to its purpose; in no other period or place has armor ever been developed so perfectly adapted in beauty of form, dignity and suitability. The beginning of the Renaissance coincided with the full flowering of the Gothic age, and the armor of the period is notable, among other things for its exquisite decoration, which was produced by etching, gilding, and chasing over a plate base that was often forged with consummate skill into beautiful flutings and other patterns.

A considerable part of the refinement of form derived from close attention to the functions performed by each half of the body: the left was the half of the bridle arm used to control the armored knight's horse, while the right was the lance or sword arm used for

An open burgonet of the type favored by light horsemen in the 16th century in preference to the more protective but also more weighty close helmet.

Etched half armor of the
North Italian school, about
1575, with a peaked morion.

The longest recorded ride in 112-lb full armor was achieved by Dick Brown between Edinburgh and Dumfries in Scotland. Brown covered 167 miles in a riding time of 28 hours and 30 minutes between June 13 and 15, 1979.

Mary, Queen of Scots, is led to her execution by a gentleman wearing a typical breastplate of the day. The preceding escort are wearing half armor and combed morions.

North Italian half armor made
between 1570 and 1580.

fighting. The earlier symmetrical armor gave way to the Gothic, whose asymmetrical appearance reflected the different roles of the body's two halves. The breastplate was made of two or more overlapping parts that met in a point and were connected by leather straps or rivets to give a measure of flexibility. The shoulder and elbow cops were made large enough to provide complete protection for these important joints; the hands were protected by mitten gauntlets; and the feet were protected by laminated solerets (armor "shoes" with long, pointed toes that could be removed when the rider dismounted.) Great attention was given to the plate itself, which was of marvelous quality and varied in thickness to provide exactly the desired protective and load-carrying capabilities. The weight of the complete ensemble was inevitably great; this placed emphasis on tailoring not only the thickness of the various plates, but also the various parts of individual plates.

Just as the heaume had been replaced by the lighter basinet, the latter in turn gave way to the "chapel de fer" and the "salade." The chapel de fer (iron hat) was an open helmet that had first appeared in the 12th century largely for foot soldiers, but which enjoyed increasing popularity for mounted knights from the early 15th century. It was considerably lighter than the

Horse armor is properly known as bardings, and generally developed alongside the armor for its riders, using a mix of boiled leather, chain mail, and steel for the protection of the horse's head, neck, chest, and hind quarters.

An Italian parade casque, probably made in 1530 by Filippo Negroli of Milan.

41

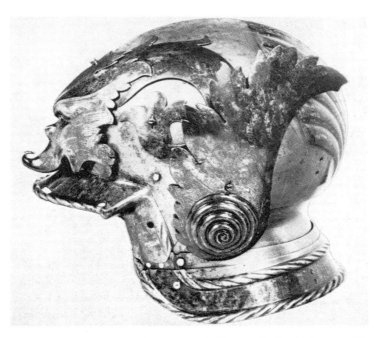

A German parade casque, made in about 1530 by Koloman Helmschmied of Augsburg.

basinet, and in its developed forms, it had deep side and rear skirts that offered considerable protection against sweeping and descending blows. The salade was a development of the chapel de fer, offering greater protection by a deepening of the down-turned brim and the provision of frontal protection as far down as the nostrils. The salade appears to have been developed in two different forms, as the German salade and Italian barbute or celata. The German type was close to the head at the front and sides, but then stretched out at the rear in a long pointed boat tail; the front was fitted with an upward-pivoting visor, or was solid with an eye slit. English and French salades were generally similar to the German pattern, except for their shorter tails. The Italian type fitted more closely around the entire head like the helmet of ancient Greece. It sometimes left the wearer's face completely exposed, but was generally solid with a large T-shaped cutout.

The Gothic pattern of armor lasted well into the 16th century. The main developments were the widespread use of fluting in the plate, the provision of large ridges over the upper part of the breastplate and around the armpits, and the adoption of better-articulated joints. The last remain classic examples of the metalsmith's art, demonstrating the use of many small plates beautifully forged and fitted together to provide ample movement while omitting the large guards previously essential over the joints.

This refined Gothic pattern of basic armor was completed by yet another type of helmet, the "armet," which provided greater protection than the salade, but was lighter. The armet first appeared in the third

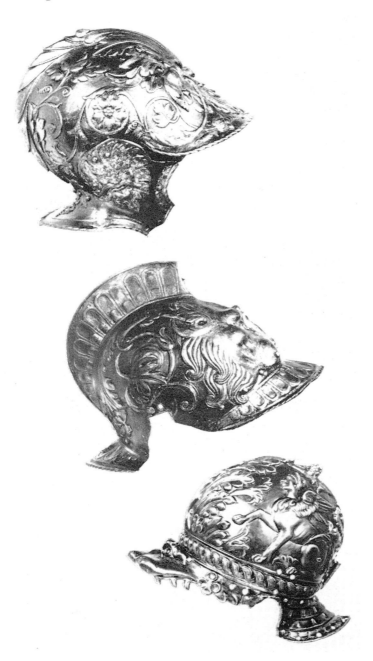

From the beginning of the 15th century, shields were fitted with a bouche (mouth) in the upper righthand corner so that the lance could be aimed without exposing the knight's body.

Italian 16th century parade casques.

43

quarter of the 15th century, and was a close-fitting helmet that protected the face, head, and neck. The armet reflects the development of the metalsmith's skills in the period, for it fitted so closely around the head that it had to be opened out before it could be put on. In early armets, cheek pieces were hinged from a point just below the visor pivots, closing in front of the wearer's chin in a joint that was protected by the

A 15th century war chariot in the period when gunpowder weapons co-existed well with bows and blade weapons: the men are wearing half-armor and war hats.

44

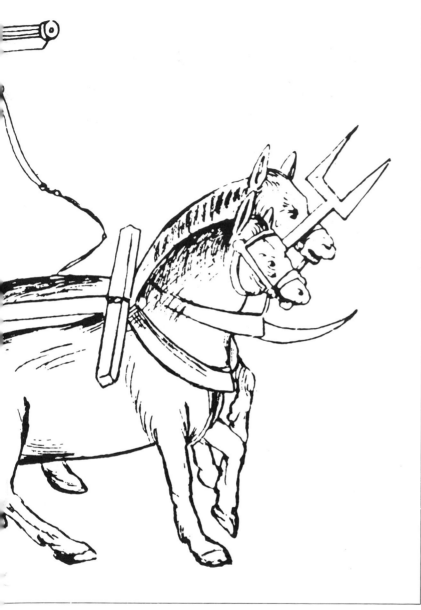

lowered visor. This continental pattern was replaced by an English type that fitted even more closely to the head and had a one-section chinpiece pivoting on the same lugs as the visor. The original armet was supported by the head, but the addition of a deep gorget around the base gave additional protection to the neck and upper chest while allowing the shoulders to carry the main burden. The gorget was sometimes made as

a separate section onto which the armet fitted to allow the wearer to turn his head. The armet was used all over Europe by the beginning of the 16th century, and remained in use for about a century.

The combination of fluted Gothic body armor and the armet produced an overall pattern of armor known as the Maximilian, which lasted from 1500 to 1540. It is generally associated with fluting that radiated from the center of the breastplate, rounded outlines, and blunt-

Far left: A richly decorated gorget made in Milan about 1610.

Left: Full man and horse armor of the etched, blued and gilt type.

47

Below: A peaked morion, made in Italy about 1580.

tipped sabatons rather than pointed solerets for the feet. The Maximilian gave way to the full flowering of a Gothic pattern of extraordinary complexity and beauty of ornamentation, constructed from a larger number of more carefully forged parts. The strength of the armor was still enormous, but the degree of ornamentation was a hindrance to the armor's use in battle: the embossing, etching, and gilding removed the homogeneous smooth exterior of the armor, creating a surface of contrasting materials and pockets that allowed lances and sword blades to catch in them.

Right: Decorated half-armor and burgonet.

48

49

Claude Louis Hector,
Duc de Villars (1653-1734)
wearing arm and upper leg
armor.

To a large extent, this increasing ornamentation reflects the decreasing importance of armor. Body and horse armor were incredibly expensive, and could only be bought by the wealthiest classes. Yet, in the Battle of Crécy (1346), at the cost of only about 100 men, the archers of Edward III's English army killed 4,000 men out of a total French force of 12,000: most were noblemen, and their decisive defeat at the hands of low-born archers indicated that a complete change was coming in the social balance of Europe. This lesson was reinforced in the Battle of Agincourt (1415), when the 5,000 archers of Henry V's 6,000-man English army routed 20,000 French troops under the Constable d'Albret: the English suffered about 1,600 casualties, but left the French with at least 7,000 dead and wounded. What the bow started, the handgun completed, for, with such a weapon, even an unskilled man could defeat an armored knight without difficulty.

The threat posed by the gun in the 16th century became acute as the century progressed. The armored knight could not carry enough protection to ensure his safety from the gun, so the only possible solution was to concentrate the weight (and therefore the thickness) over the man's most vulnerable areas. As parade or ceremonial armor became more ornamental and less practical, battle armor became simpler, but clumsier because of its thicker plate. During

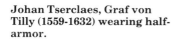

Johan Tserclaes, Graf von Tilly (1559-1632) wearing half-armor.

The manteau d'armes was a fixed shield with a specially roughened surface. It was worn in 16th century tournaments with the object of catching the opponent's lance head and breaking the lance or unseating its owner.

Right: Parts of horse armor in the forms (*top*) of a French saddle steel (covering the front and back of the saddle) from about 1580, (*center*) a pair of Milanese saddle steels dating from about 1550, and (*bottom*) an embossed and damascened circular plaque of the 16th century.

Far right: A combed morion of the German type, probably made in Nuremberg in 1580.

the 16th century, battle armor gradually lost its completeness. The sections below the knees were the first to go, then the arm sections; the thigh sections were shortened, the closed helmet disappeared in favor of a lighter open type, the backplate was abandoned, and finally the breastplate was given up. All that was left

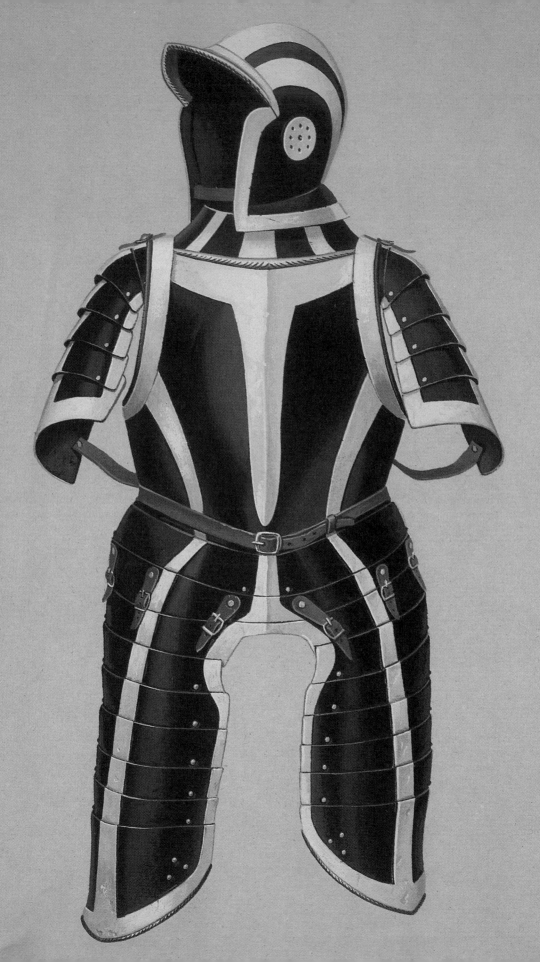

Left: European stirrups from the period 1560-1600.

was the gorget and, occasionally, the helmet. By 1650, the knight and his armor had disappeared from European battlefields. The only remnants of armor were breastplates and helmets for the cavalry, and to a certain extent, for foot soldiers such as pikemen.

Running parallel to battle armor and its elaborate parade equivalent was tournament armor. The two "combat" types were basically the same until the end of the 14th century, when the particular circumstances of the tournament led to a slightly different strain of development. In the 15th century, ordinary armor was frequently modified for tournament use by the addition of strengthening plates laced over the outside of the suit, but there was an increasing tendency toward specialized tournament armor, reflecting the fact that opponents rode against each other in exactly the same

Far left: Cut-down half-armor of the late 16th century, the elimination of all the lower arm and much of the shoulder protection indicating how armor evolved towards maneuverability and lightness once the threat of gunpowder weapons had been fully appreciated.

The lives of knights were too important to be risked unnecessarily in tournaments from the 16th century onward, and the head of tilting lances was therefore fitted with a coronal, a rounded metal head with three blunt points to catch in the opponent's armor and unhorse him.

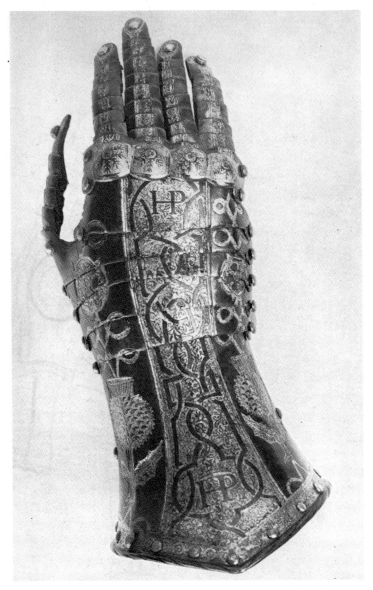

A gauntlet made by William Pickering at Greenwich in about 1612 for Henry, Prince of Wales.

fashion and at the same angle each time. The breastplate was often of the so-called "box" type, projecting on the right to support a resting place for the heavy lance, the helmet was firmly fixed (often bolted) to it. The helmet was very different from the battle type, and was really a heavy version of the heaulme with only a small vision slit and emphasis on deflecting the lance. The barrier down the center of the list generally protected the riders below the waist, and many suits of tournament armor had nothing below the waist except thigh pieces, while others relied on plates fastened to

"Dress" armor of the late 16th century.

57

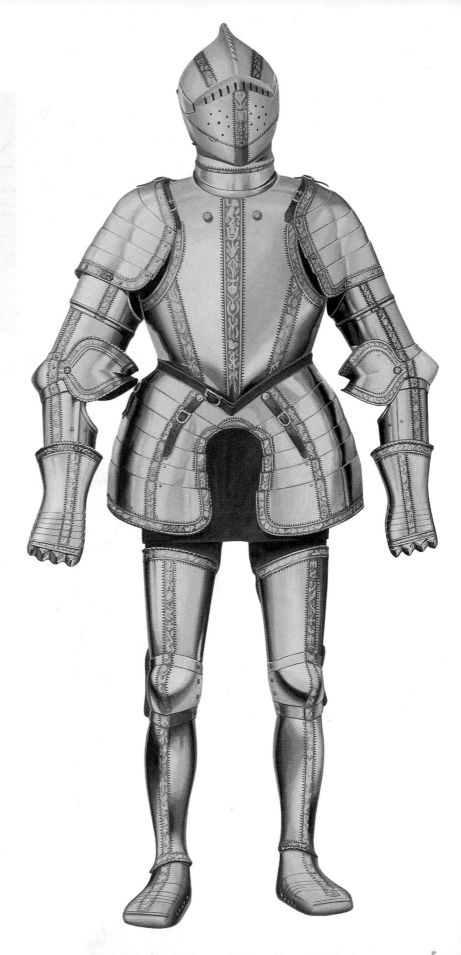

For extra protection and decoration in tilts, knights often wore an escuffa, which was a plate covering the top and back of the head. It was often pierced for lightness, and worn over the standard helmet of the period.

Full plate armor was in its heyday a marvel of the metalsmith's skill in hand-forging the many individual pieces and then assembling them into a suit of such fine articulation that the wearer could not only move but fight in it.

French and German or
Flemish bucklers (small
shields) of embossed steel, all
made in the period from 1570
to 1590.

the saddle to protect the legs. Tournaments were
organized in many forms, and knights with a special
interest in tournaments sometimes possessed a special
core suit to which as many 100 pieces could be added
to create exactly the right suit for any particular tournament.

Even after the gun had made armor completely
obsolete, some of its elements survived: cavalry

Definitive plate armor showing the full articulation and protection that could be achieved with an almost miraculous skill by European armorers in the 16th century.

troops, for example, continued to use the sword for many years after it had disappeared from the foot soldier's armory, and a breastplate and helmet therefore continued to be worn against the slashing attack of a saber, with a marginal capability against the lance still carried by light cavalry. Such armor is still worn as part of the ceremonial uniforms of units such as the Household Cavalry of the British establishment, and a last remnant of the foot soldier's armor survives in the small gorget worn by men serving as provosts.

"Spanish" morions (with narrow brims and less pointed tops) and burgonets made in France, Germany and Italy in the 16th and 17th centuries.

Glossary

Ailette: shoulder protection

Armet: lightened version of the salade offering close protection of the head and face

Armor: personal protection against shock and, to a lesser extent, missile weapons

Backplate: plate protection for the back

Barbuta: Italian version of the salade

Barrel helm: helmet of basically cylindrical shape with a flat top

Basinet: replacement for the great helm, providing less protection but offering lighter weight and greater maneuverability

Box breastplate: type of breastplate with inbuilt support for the lance

Breastplate: plate protection for the chest and stomach

Brigandine armor: armor comprising outer layers of cloth or leather over a central layer of plates or rings

Camail: chain mail protection for the back of the neck

Celata: alternative name for barbuta

Chapel de fer: lighted version of the basinet with deeper side and neck pieces for added protection of these vulnerable areas

Cop: knee protection, generally of boiled leather

Corselet: mail or plate protection for the chest and stomach

Embossing: decoration of plate by stamping patterns or motifs on it

Etching: decoration of plate by removing some of the outer surface to leave a pattern or motif

Gambeson: quilted garment worn under a hauberk

Gilding: decoration of etched plate by filling removed portions of the outer surface with gold.

Gorget: protection for the front of the neck and upper chest

Great helm: fully developed from the sugar-loaf helm

Greave: plate armor protection for the shins

Hauberk: mail coat with sleeves

Helmet: a "hat" to protect the head from downward and sideways attack, in its formal sense made with a pointed top

Lance: knight's primary weapon at the beginning of battle or tournament, a long spear that was carried by a horsed knight for thrusting rather than throwing.

Mail armor: an evolution of brigandine armor comprising small rings interlinked with each other and generally attached to the outer surface of a quilted inner garment.

Missile weapon: one that is thrown or projected

Nasal: downward protection from the helmet to protect the wearer's nose

Plate armor: armor made of plate metal rather than interlinked rings

Pot helmet: simple curved-top device to protect the head

Ring armor: precursor of mail armor, in which individual rings were attached to the undergarment but not linked together.

Sabaton: blunt-tipped amored shoe

Salade: version of the chapel de fer providing better protection for the cheeks

Shield: variously shaped protective device carried on one arm to ward off blows against the head, chest and stomach

Shock weapon: one that is wielded by a man to hit his opponent directly

Solaret: point-tipped armored shoe

Sugar-loaf helm: evolution of the barrel helm with a pointed top

Tournament armor: armor specially designed and made for tournaments (fighting competitions) rather than battle

Visor: protection for the wearer's face and eyes, generally comprising a panel hinged so that it could be lifted or turned out of the way when not needed

Index